Winning Shopping Center Designs No.6

Visual Reference Publications, Inc.
New York

Visual Reference Publications, Inc.
302 Fifth Avenue
New York, NY 10001

Distributors to the trade in the United States and Canada
Watson-Guptill
1515 Broadway
New York, NY 10036

Distributors outside the United States and Canada
Hearst Books International
1350 Avenue of the Americas
New York, NY 10019

Book Design: Harish Patel Design Associates, New York

Library of Congress Cataloging in Publication Data:
Winning Shopping Center Designs No.6

Printed in Hong Kong
ISBN 1-58471-003-9

Contents

INNOVATIVE DESIGN
AND CONSTRUCTION OF
A NEW PROJECT

Foreword		**5**
Acknowledgments		**5**
About the ICSC International Design and Development Awards		**6**

Brass Mill Center, Waterbury, Connecticut, USA   **9**
Owner: General Growth Properties, Inc.
Architect/Designer: Arrowstreet Inc.

Centro Colombo, Lisbon, Portugal   **17**
Owner: Empreendimentos Imobiliarios Colombo, S.A.
Architect: Jose Quintela Da Fonseca
Designer: RTKL Associates Inc.

Redmond Town Center   **25**
Redmond, Washington, USA
Owner: The Macerich Company
Architect/Designer: LMN Architects

Santa Margarita Town Center   **33**
Rancho Santa Margarita, California, USA
Owner: Koll Development Company
Architect/Designer: Altoon + Porter Architects

Arizona Mills, Tempe, Arizona, USA   **41**
Owner: Arizona Mills L.L.C.
Architect/Designer: JPRA Architects

The Avenue at White Marsh   **49**
Baltimore, Maryland, USA
Owner: Nottingham Properties, Inc.
Architect/Designer: RTKL Associates Inc.

Centerra Marketplace   **57**
Lebanon, New Hampshire, USA
Owner: Dartmouth College Real Estate Inc.
Architect/Designer: Arrowstreet Inc.

Glendale Marketplace   **65**
Glendale, California, USA
Owner: Glendale Marketplace, LLC
Architect/Designer: Feola, Carli & Archuleta

Main Place, Naperville, Illinois, USA   **73**
Owner: The Rubin Jefferson Partnership
Architect/Designer: MCG Architecture

The Mall, Cribbs Causeway, Bristol, UK   **81**
Owner: The Prudential Assurance Co. Ltd. and
JT Baylis & Co. Ltd.
Architect/Designer: Building Design Partnership

Viejas Outlet Center 89
Alpine, California, USA

Owner: Viejas Tribal Council
Architect: Sollberg + Lowe
Designer: Bullock, Smith & Partners

Yokohama Bayside Marina Shops and Restaurants 97
Yokohama, Kanagawa-Ken, Japan

Owner: Mitsui Fudosan Co. Ltd.
Architect: Mitsui Construction Co. Ltd.
Designer: RTKL Associates Inc.

RENOVATION OR
EXPANSION OF AN
EXISTING PROJECT

Cavendish Square 105
Claremont, Cape Town, South Africa

Owner: Old Mutual Properties
Architect/Designer: Development Design Group, Inc.

Fashion Valley Center 113
San Diego, California, USA

Owner: Equitable Asset Management
Architect/Designer: Altoon + Porter Architects

Bangor Mall, Bangor, Maine, USA 121

Owner: Banmak Associates
Architect/Designer: Arrowstreet Inc.

Beachwood Place, Beachwood, Ohio, USA 129

Owner: The Rouse Company
Architect/Designer: RTKL Associates Inc.

The Manteca Marketplace 137
Manteca, California, USA

Owner: The Canada Life Assurance Company
Architect: Ty Miller, Architect
Designer: Chase Parker Corporation

Northwoods Cafe at Fox River Center 145
Appleton, Wisconsin, USA

Owner: General Growth Properties
Architect/Designer Anthony Belluschi Architects, Ltd.

Oak Park Mall 153
Overland Park, Kansas, USA

Owner: Oak Park Investments, L.P.
c/o Copaken, White & Blitt
Architect: HNTB Corp.
Designer: RTKL Associates Inc.

Raffles City Shopping Centre, Singapore 161

Owner: Raffles City Pte. Ltd.
Architect: Architects 61 Pte. Ltd.
Designer: RTKL International Ltd.

Shopping Center Iguatemi Porto Alegre Expansion 169
Porto Alegre, RS, Brazil

Owner: Iguatemi Empresa de Shopping Centers SA,
Nacional Iguatemi Ancar, Maiojama
Architect/Designer: Beame Architectural Partnership

Foreword

The dramatic growth of shopping centers in the 1960s and 1970s reflected the young industry's ability to provide new shopping experiences for the rapidly expanding consumer market. The initial developments were simple in layout and design. Over time, shopping centers have become more sophisticated, varied and complex, as owners continued to provide new shopping and entertainment experiences for customers with dramatically increasing choices.

While today's shopping center industry is truly international, the retail challenges are similar in most markets — competitive shopping centers, on-line (or catalog) shopping, alternative forms of entertainment and a sensory-overloaded public. When combined with current economic realities, today's shopping center developers and owners must be innovative and disciplined to succeed.

The worldwide recognition of outstanding projects forms the basis of the ICSC International Design and Development Awards Program. ICSC's historic standard of excellence was reflected this year in the six Design Award winners and fifteen Certificate of Merit recipients. International entries included projects in Portugal, South Africa, Brazil, Singapore, United Kingdom and Japan. U.S. projects ranged from a new 50,000 square-foot strip center in Naperville, Illinois, to a 1.7 million square-foot remodel/expansion in San Diego, California.

The International Design and Development Awards Jury Committee is composed of nine industry leaders from development, retailing, architecture and consulting firms. They average in excess of twenty years' experience each and invest hours in judging each year's submissions. I am grateful to them for their dedication and professionalism.

This book presents the winning submissions in this year's 23rd International Design and Development Awards Program. We hope it inspires future projects, striving to provide new shopping and entertainment experiences.

Daryl K. Mangan
Cole Vision Corporation

Chairman
ICSC 1999 International Design and Development Awards Jury Committee

About the ICSC International Design and Development Awards

The ICSC International Design and Development Awards Program was established to recognize outstanding shopping center projects and to provide information on them to the entire industry so that others may benefit from the experiences of their colleagues.

The 23rd International Design and Development Awards Program was worldwide in scope. Participation in other ICSC Design Awards Programs, such as the Canadian or European Awards, did not preclude eligible projects from being considered for an International Design and Development Award.

Projects which opened within the 18-month period, January 1, 1997, to June 30, 1998, were eligible for entry into this year's Awards Program.

Awards Categories

Categories for entries were:

Category A—Renovation or Expansion of an Existing Project
Entries had to relate to a project involving an entire shopping center, such as an enclosure, or a single facet of a center, such as an addition. The renovation or expansion must have been completed and the center fully opened for business within the 18-month period, January 1, 1997, to June 30, 1998. Eligible subject matter included, but was not limited to, improving the use of existing space, methods of keeping a center open during construction, new marketing and re-leasing approaches, refinancing techniques, innovative design and construction approaches, and adaptive reuse of the structure.

Category B—Innovative Design and Construction of a New Project
Entries had to relate to a specific new shopping center, completed and opened within the 18-month period, January 1, 1997, to June 30, 1998, and must have demonstrated how a specific design or construction problem was solved or how new standards in design or construction were established. New methods of environmental enhancement, space utilization design themes, energy conservation and innovative construction techniques were among the subjects that were considered for this category. Entries included detailed information about the

design and construction of the center, such as explanations of the reasons for, and the realized accomplishments of, the particular approach.

Awards Classifications

Entries submitted for either **category** were judged according to the following center **classification** system:

1. Projects under 150,000 square feet of total retail space*

2. Projects of 150,001 to 500,000 square feet of total retail space*

3. Projects over 500,001 square feet of total retail space.*

*Total retail space includes all square footage included in gross leasable areas (GLA), all department store or other anchor square footage, movie theaters, ice skating rinks, entertainment centers, and all peripheral (out-lot) space engaged in retail enterprise. It does not include office or hotel square footage.

Eligibility

1. The ICSC International Design and Development Awards Program was open only to ICSC member companies. Any ICSC member company could enter as many projects as desired in either of the two categories.

2. Entries must have had the authorization and signature of the owner or management company of the property.

3. Projects opened within the 18-month period, January 1, 1997 to June 30, 1998, were eligible.

4. Projects must have been completed and opened for business by June 30, 1998.

5. Separate phases of a project could be submitted individually, provided they were completed and opened for business by June 30, 1998.

6. Projects could only be submitted once. Projects that were entered in the past could not be resubmitted unless substantial changes were made since the last submission.

7. Members entering the ICSC Canadian or ICSC European Awards Programs had to submit separately to the International Design and Development Awards Program, and entries had to adhere to its entry guidelines and requirements. Entries accepted to other ICSC awards programs did not automatically qualify for this program, nor was any entry excluded simply because it was an award winner in another program.

If you have any questions about the International Council of Shopping Centers International Design and Development Awards, or would like to receive an application for the upcoming awards program, please write or call:

International Council of Shopping Centers
International Design and Development Awards
665 Fifth Avenue
New York, NY 10022-5370
Telephone: (212) 421-8181, ext. 320
FAX: (212) 486-0849

Acknowledgments

The International Council of Shopping Centers 23rd International Design and Development Awards were selected by a committee of diverse shopping center professionals representing retailers, developers and architects. The International Council of Shopping Centers is grateful to these judges for the time, effort and expertise they contributed to the awards program.

Daryl K. Mangan, *Chairman*
Cole Vision Corporation
Twinsburg, Ohio

Ronald A. Altoon, FAIA
Altoon + Porter Architects
Los Angeles, California

Stanley C. Burgess
The Rouse Company
Columbia, Maryland

F. Carl Dieterle, Jr.
Simon Property Group
Indianapolis, Indiana

Gordon T. Greeby
GCI-ProNet Midwest
Lake Bluff, Illinois

John Millar, CSM
General Growth Properties
Chicago, Illinois

Rao K. Sunku
JC Penney Co., Inc.
Dallas, Texas

Ian F. Thomas
Thomas Consultants, Inc.
Vancouver, British Columbia

Gerald M. White
Copaken, White & Blitt
Leawood, Kansas

Owner:
General Growth Properties, Inc.
Chicago, Illinois, United States

Architect/Designer:
Arrowstreet Inc.
Somerville, Massachusetts, United States

Brass Mill Center
Waterbury, Connecticut, United States

Gross size of center:
989,382 sq. ft.

Gross leasable area excluding anchors:
399,791 sq. ft.

Total acreage of site:
64.1 acres

Type of center:
Regional center

Physical description:
Enclosed two-level mall, with third-level cinema

Location of trading area:
Urban but not downtown

Population:
- Primary trading area
  339,600
- Secondary trading area
  600,000
- Annualized percentage of shoppers anticipated to be from outside trade area
  30%

Development schedule:
- Original opening date
  September 17, 1997

Parking spaces:
- Present number
  4,637

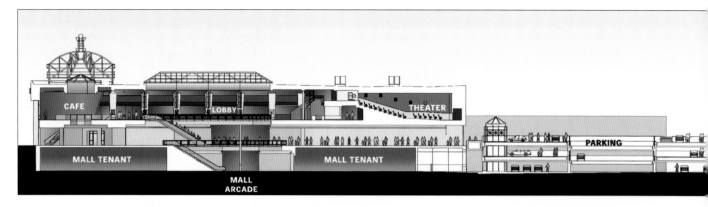

Moviegoers to the third-floor theater travel through the retail areas to reach the cinema lobby.

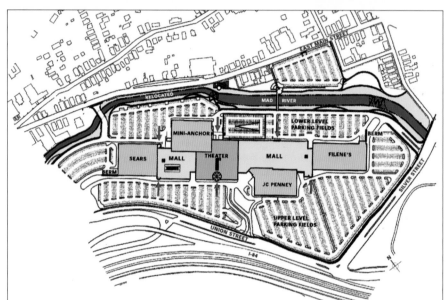

Site work brought environmental enhancements, including a greenbelt alongside the relocated Mad River.

*B*rass Mill Center stands on what had been an unsightly stretch of abandoned factory land. An inventive partnership between its developers, federal and state governments, and community groups transformed the brown field into a two-level enclosed mall topped by a third-level cinema. Prior to construction, the area required substantial site spoils removal and replacement — up to 20 percent of the site contained soils contaminated with hazardous materials. To create a site large enough, about 1,000 linear feet of the Mad River was culverted, and another 1,000 relocated, in concert with local roads. State agencies worked with the developer to clean up the river to promote passage for fish needing to spawn upstream, restoring activity to the area's ecosystem. A mile-long pedestrian park was built along the river. In all, the state and federal governments invested $36 million in the site clean up. As a result 3,300 mall-related jobs came to Waterbury, which had the highest unemployment rate in the state.

MAJOR TENANTS		
NAME	**TYPE**	**GLA (SQ. FT.)**
Filene's	Department store	165,000
Sears	Department store	150,140
JC Penney	Department store	126,114
Hoyts	Multiscreen cinema	70,499

Prior to development, abandoned buildings like the rolling shed were community eyesores.

The building itself has an industrial design theme, in keeping with Waterbury's manufacturing heritage. An open-dome crown structure over the main entry projects the design statement to approaching shoppers. At the pedestrian scale, the industrial motif is reinforced by etched-glass and laser-cut steel railing designs, by inventive brass ventilation grills and by commemorative brass floor plaques. Signage and environmental graphics also reflect the factory concept.

Approaching shoppers get the first hint of the industrial design theme from the open-dome crown structure over the mall.

Among the targets for environmental improvement was this industrial canal section of the Mad River, which became a part of a thriving riverfront walk. Public-private partnership in the Mad River realignment (below) made the water safe for fish and created a pleasant environment for pedestrians.

The center's illuminated crown (opposite) beckons to the highway at night, with the theater lobby visible.

At the three-story center court, colorful waterjet-cut floor tiles form a mosaic that recalls clock faces and brass machinery parts. The curved main arcade trusses, which clear-span 45 feet across the mall, recall the roof structures in the brass rolling sheds that once occupied the site.

According to the developer, placing of a 12-screen multiplex on the third level was a last-minute leasing and design concept. The prominence of the theater seen from the highway became an important advertising feature for the mall. Theater patrons enter through mall entrances and circulate through the retail arcade before and after a show. About 2 million moviegoers walk the mall and eat at the restaurants and large food court.

The three-story center court includes an elevator and coffee bar. A secondary mall entrance, inspired by the city's many towers, repeats the crown motif.

The industrial design motif is seen in glass-etched railing designs, the food court ceiling gears, brass floor tiles, return-air grills and mall signage.

Placing the theater above the mall required transferring the building's structural loads. A skylight in the cinema's ceiling and a large well opening in the cinema's lobby floor allow natural light to beam into the mall levels below. The synergy between cinema entertainment, food and shopping has energized Brass Mill Center and provided a new front door for Waterbury.

The view from the cinema lobby to two levels of the mall arcade demonstrates the energy of Brass Mill Center.

Owner:

Empreendimentos Imobiliarios Colombo, S.A.
Lisbon, Portugal

Architect:

Jose Quintela Da Fonseca
Lisbon, Portugal

Designer:

RTKL Associates Inc.
Dallas, Texas, United States

Centro Colombo

Lisbon, Portugal

Gross size of center:
2,000,000 sq. ft.

Gross leasable area excluding anchors:
357,597 sq. ft.

Total acreage of site:
20 acres

Type of center:
Super-regional center

Physical description:
Enclosed mall

Location of trading area:
Urban but not downtown

Population:
- Primary trading area
  495,000
- Secondary trading area
  1,375,000
- Annualized percentage of shoppers
  anticipated to be from outside trade area
  20%

Development schedule:
- Original opening date
  September 16, 1997

Parking spaces:
- Present number
  6,800

Towering vestibules welcome shoppers to Centro Colombo.

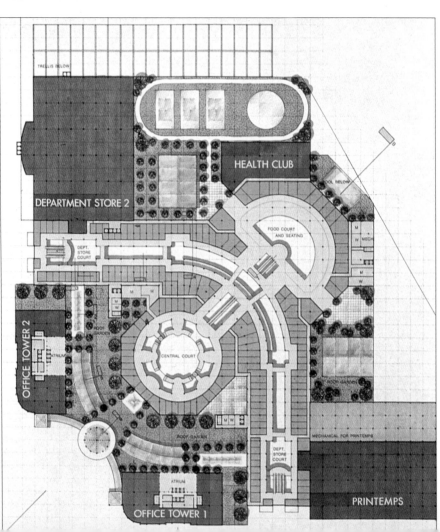

*U*nique among Europe's malls, a large family entertainment center at Centro Colombo calls out to tourists as well as residents of Portugal's capital.

Located on the outskirts of Lisbon, Portugal, Centro Colombo is part of a mixed-use development that will include two 17-story office towers, a four-star hotel and three levels of underground parking.

The panoramic sweep of the center is evident at dusk (left) and by day (below).

The shopping center itself includes department stores, more then 500 retail shops, a hypermarket and a 10-screen cinema. Its food court contains 60 eateries and has a seating capacity for 1,200 diners. While more than 300 shops are Portuguese, the remainder reflect other nations' retailers and lend Centro Colombo a truly international flavor.

Even with these superlatives, for many the center's highlight is its third-level entertainment area, which contains a 24-lane bowling alley, roller coaster, merry-go-round, virtual-reality arcade and a go-cart track. The play center also includes a health club with squash courts, a swimming pool, a golfing area and a jogging track on the roof.

MAJOR TENANTS		
NAME	TYPE	GLA (SQ. FT.)
Hypermarket Continente	Supermarket	317,415
Play Center	Recreation area	129,000
Warner Multiplex	Multiscreen cinema	55,390
Marks & Spencer	Department store	45,509
CMA	Department store	41,053
SF/Snac	Department store	40,418

A tall atrium topped by strong graphics draws the eye to upper-level retail shops, while water features enhance the pedestrian area.

The interior design is inspired by the country's nautical past and draws upon historic Portuguese and Moorish detailing. Shoppers are drawn to the center's terra-cotta-colored public squares, formal arcades and classical rotundas. Designs for these areas are derived from traditional Portuguese town squares. Modern amenities, such as walls lined with videoscreens, coexist comfortably alongside the native design elements.

The developer says the center was built through the largest private long-term financing in the history of Portugal, provided by the nation's six largest banks. The national and international impact of Centro Colombo — the largest mall on the Iberian peninsula — is evident in numbers: each month, 410,000 cars enter the grounds, 450,000 shoppers arrive via the metro linking the center to central Lisbon and 500,000 people visit the entertainment center.

Visibility of stores at all levels (left) is one key to attracting customers.

Nautical references such as fish and dolphins (this page) and sextants (opposite, below) remind visitors of the nation's heritage.

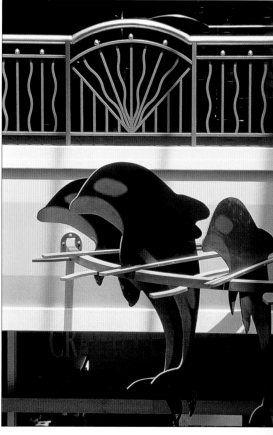

Over 30 million customers — roughly three times the population of Portugal — visited Centro Colombo its first year, demonstrating that entertainment and retail can be successfully integrated, even at a good distance from the nearest major city.

Palm trees and natural light punctuate the strong graphic elements of the center court.

Owner:

The Macerich Company

Santa Monica, California, United States

Architect/Designer:

LMN Architects

Seattle, Washington, United States

Redmond Town Center

Redmond, Washington, United States

Gross size of center:
700,000 sq. ft.

Gross leasable area excluding anchors:
375,000 sq. ft.

Total acreage of site:
40 acres

Type of center:
Regional fashion/specialty center

Physical description:
Open mall

Location of trading area:
Urban but not downtown

Population:
- Primary trading area
  200,000
- Secondary trading area
  150,000
- Annualized percentage of shoppers
  anticipated to be from outside trade area
  10%

Development schedule:
- Original opening date
  September 1997
- Current expansion date
  September 1998

Parking spaces:
- Present number
  2,800

Parking areas at Redmond Town Center are often surrounded by retail buildings, making storefront windows visible to pedestrians.

Photo: Skyview Aerial Survey

*T*he design of Redmond Town Center in Washington State harmonizes the center, the environment and the adjacent downtown. The site, a former golf course, contains two salmon-bearing waterways and hundreds of mature firs. The site master plan, developed over many months, preserved those resources by establishing significant buffers and saving nearly 70 percent of the wooded portions of the site. The city's Farmer's Market was incorporated into the plan as well.

Photo: Eckert & Eckert

Photo: John A. Gallagher

A pylon makes design reference to the salmon in nearby streams.

The extensive use of brick in the design is evident in a plaza (left) and building columns and facades (below).

Creative signage points the way to the parking area.

Photos: John A. Gallagher

The center is part of a planned mixed-use project, which will include office, public, hotel and residential buildings. Planning, which involved fourteen permits from city, county, state and federal agencies, extended the city's street grid system into the site. Rather than a huge, enclosed, inward-facing mall, the development is divided into city-size blocks containing individual buildings that support pedestrian activity. Street-level facades have storefront windows, canopies and rich materials that can be appreciated by pedestrians.

MAJOR TENANTS

NAME	TYPE	GLA (SQ. FT.)
Cineplex Odeon	Multiscreen cinema	38,858
Limited Stores	Fashion/Apparel	35,000
REI	Apparel/Recreation	35,000
Borders Books	Books/Music	25,535
Z Gallerie	Home furnishings	25,151
Eddie Bauer	Fashion	23,186

Shaded plazas (below and overleaf) unify Redmond Town Center with surrounding city life.

Photo: Eckert & Eckert

As a design concept, the owner, architect and city planners agreed on an image best seen in some of the original 1920 brick buildings in the Old Town District of Redmond. The richness and detailing of these buildings inspired the design decision to use brick and other masonry materials. Brick and precast concrete cover beam spandrels and storefront and arcade columns.

A particular challenge was to place parking in an area where it would be out of sight, or at least provide minimal visibility. The three-level main parking structure was therefore located in the interior of the block, with buildings wrapped around it on three sides. Instead of parking lots, pedestrians see three distinct outdoor plazas, which have become gathering places for

Water features sparkle by day (below), while dusk brings imaginative use of overhead lighting.

Photos: Eckert & Eckert (opposite and above); John A. Gallagher (right).

Photo: John A. Gallagher

Retailing coexists well with the automobile on the citylike streets of Redmond Town Center.

Photo: Eckert & Eckert

residents and shop employees. The plazas contain exposed steel-truss canopy structures and are carpeted with the color and texture of concrete pavers on both walking and driving surfaces.

The developer sees the partnership with city government as the key to making the project a success. In all, Winmar Company contributed $6 million in off-site improve-ments to the city's transportation system and utility infrastructure, including 1.4 miles of public streets, utility improve-ments and a sewer lift station.

Owner:

Koll Development Company
Newport Beach, California, United States

Architect/Designer:

Altoon + Porter Architects
Los Angeles, California, United States

Santa Margarita Town Center

Rancho Santa Margarita, California, United States

Gross size of center:
310,000 sq. ft.

Gross leasable area excluding anchors:
201,000 sq. ft.

Total acreage of site:
29 acres

Type of center:
Community center

Physical description:
Strip center

Location of trading area:
Suburban

Population:
- Primary trading area
  200,000
- Secondary trading area
  350,000
- Annualized percentage of shoppers anticipated to be from outside trade area
  5%

Development schedule:
- Original opening date
  Winter 1997
- Future expansion
  2000

Parking spaces:
- Present number
  1,890
- 1,500 parking spaces to be added

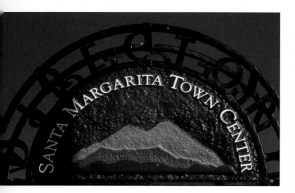

Santa Margarita Town Center combines retailing and the community life of a master-planned residential area. The developers had the obligation to tie into a legislated open-space framework that links the residential neighborhoods to open-space resources and the local public school. The requirements mandated a Mediterranean-style architecture and "environmentally sensitive" spaces in which the residents could congregate.

The site, excessively deep and highly exposed on multiple sides, presented design challenges in itself. Other issues came from the non-negotiable specifications of an anchor tenant, the need to avoid an elongated string of "big boxes" and the duty to link a main street, open space and the center's dining and entertainment features.

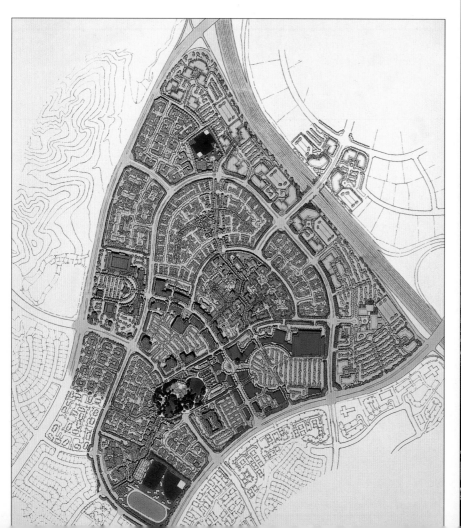

*Stores nestle
comfortably within
the landscape of
Santa Margarita
Town Center.*

The Target anchor store was located on the west end of the property, with its own parking field, vehicle access and service. The rest of Town Center was laid out around an unusual radiating layout, on which every shop can be seen from any of the four points of arrival. Thus, a project type usually designed to face freeways or major avenues was modified to allow it to nestle comfortably into its neighboring community.

Arches, palm trees, cloistered colonnades and the varied use of color create individual identities for storefronts.

MAJOR TENANTS		
NAME	TYPE	GLA (SQ. FT.)
Target	Department store	116,200
Ross Dress for Less	Clothing	27,219
Edwards Cinema	Movie theater	25,813

Tile patterning, columns and a classic setting for storefront signs tie design to regional architecture.

Against the strong form of the circular store layout, and to modify the large stucco boxes that typically house these tenants, a rich application of cloistered colonnades and trellises creates individual identities for each anchor tenant. Use of color and materials integrates the center well with the landscape.

El Paseo, the center's "main street," links Santa Margarita Town Center to nearby roads and slows traffic through the center with head-in parking. A Town Square serves as a forecourt and assembly area for the cinema and as a place for casual dining from adjacent food tenants.

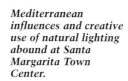

Mediterranean influences and creative use of natural lighting abound at Santa Margarita Town Center.

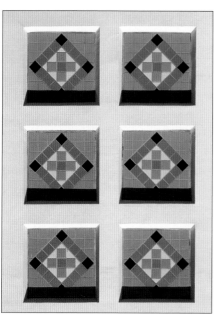

Successful linkage of retail with the surrounding town results in a shopper-friendly public space.

The developer says the project has been embraced exceptionally well by its community and is talked about in southern Orange County as "the one they did right." The center reflects the creative imagination brought to the master-planning process itself and the collaboration of the community, the landowner, the design and development teams, and the local government.

Photos: Erhard Pfeiffer

International Council of Shopping Centers
23rd International Design and Development Awards

Certificate of Merit

Innovative Design and Construction of a New Project

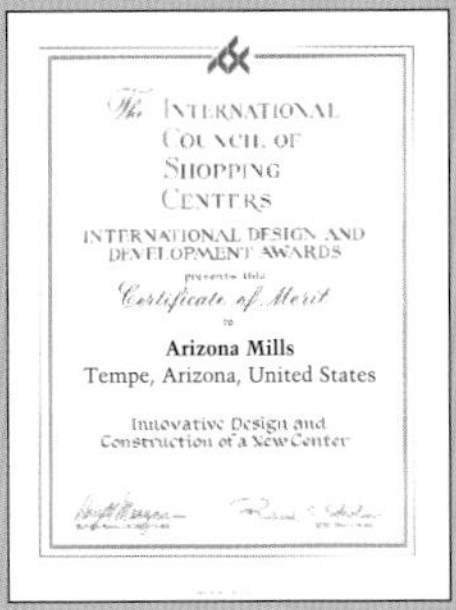

Owner:

Arizona Mills L.L.C.

Tempe, Arizona, United States

Architect/Designer:

JPRA Architects

Farmington Hills, Michigan, United States

Arizona Mills

Tempe, Arizona, United States

Gross size of center:
1,428,000 sq. ft.

Gross leasable area excluding anchors:
1,225,101 sq. ft.

Total acreage of site:
115 acres

Type of center:
Super-regional outlet center

Physical description:
Enclosed one-level mall

Location of trading area:
Suburban

Population:
- Primary trading area
  2,600,000
- Secondary trading area
  600,000
- Annualized percentage of shoppers anticipated to be from outside trade area
  35%

Development schedule:
- Original opening date
  November 20, 1997

Parking spaces:
- Present number
  6,254

*A*rizona Mills is the seventh in a line of "shoppertainment" projects developed by The Mills Corporation. Its combination of mass retailers, food and entertainment venues makes it unique within the state.

The design challenge of Arizona Mills was to develop continuity from the exterior throughout the interior, with a planned series of environmental and artistic features to achieve "retail glitter and showmanship," the developer says, and yet maintain links with the surrounding community. A further challenge was that, due to partnership agreements, the company's typical 18-month development time frame shrank to 14 months.

The exterior of traditional stucco architecture reflecting warm, neutral colors was designed to be compatible with the Arizona landscape. Art, sculpture and the natural surroundings were to entertain, guide and explain the "Arizona Mills Experience."

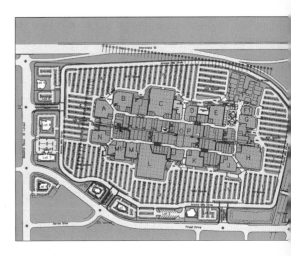

The site plan for Arizona Mills (above) shows the racetrack mall layout. At left and below, a grand-scale design structure distinguishes a mall entrance.

Exteriors of Arizona Mills show the color palette derived from the Arizona landscape.

Local artisans were involved in the initial design meetings for their input on Arizona culture and heritage and to secure their commitment to incorporate their works into the mall.

Each mall entrance contains one-of-a-kind sculptural features. Common strip wood flooring of maple and cherry is used, as is colored and stained concrete. The carpet is made up of standard colors; mixed in are the colors of the Arizona state flag. The use of over 100 colors, including many non-custom hues, makes for dramatic visuals in the center.

Each mall entry has an individual identity.

*Native-inspired art
and maple and cherry
strip-wood flooring
enhance merchandise
displays.*

An exceptional relationship with the City of Tempe and nearby communities contributed immeasurably to the center's development and identity. The developer brought municipal governments into the project early on, gaining group perspective on how to enhance the area's status as one of the world's largest vacation destinations. The City's Art in Private Development Program has generated successful partnerships between developers and artists. Arizona Mills agreed with the City of Tempe Municipal Arts Commission's mandate to "create an atmosphere in which the arts can flourish and to inspire Tempe citizens to recognize the arts as essential to the whole life of the community." The result is Arizona Mills' presentation of spirited forms, sculptural components and architecture, with such names as Wind Catcher, Magical Mystery Urns and Solquest, all in Arizona style.

MAJOR TENANTS		
NAME	TYPE	GLA (SQ. FT.)
JC Penney Outlet Store	Mass merchandiser	104,697
Harkins Theaters	Multiscreen cinema	92,320
Burlington Coat Factory	Mass merchandiser	80,426
Oshman's Supersport	Mass merchandiser	65,013

Colors, shapes and airborne forms give Arizona Mills a unique visual energy. It's partly cloudy over a tourist information booth (below, left). Videoscreens and plastic tubes overhead lend a high-tech look.

The food court air space is alive with art (below), as are the tabletops (right). An interior court (bottom) is exciting from floor to dome.

Arizona Mills is now home to about $2 million in art, and the developer says that "the luxury of more time would have enabled us to incorporate an even greater number of artists and expertise from the local community." Nonetheless, Arizona Mills demonstrates how public-private teamwork can produce a center that celebrates both retail and art.

Owner:
Nottingham Properties, Inc.
Towson, Maryland, United States

Architect/Designer:
RTKL Associates Inc.
Baltimore, Maryland, United States

The Avenue at White Marsh
Baltimore, Maryland, United States

Gross size of center:
295,981 sq. ft.

Gross leasable area excluding anchors:
221,946 sq. ft.

Total acreage of site:
34.5 acres

Type of center:
Theme/Festival center

Physical description:
One level

Location of trading area:
Suburban

Population:
- Primary trading area
  182,411
- Secondary trading area
  758,655
- Annualized percentage of shoppers
  anticipated to be from outside trade area
  20%

Development schedule:
- Original opening date
  June 13, 1998

Parking spaces:
- Present number
  2,481

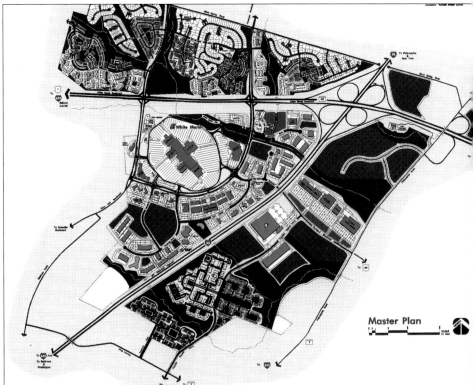

Master Plan

A high aerial view (above, top), another close-up (above) and site plan all show The Avenue at White Marsh situated in the heart of the planned community.

*T*he Avenue at White Marsh is a "main street" lifestyle retail center in the heart of White Marsh, a 2,000-acre planned community in northeastern Baltimore County. The most challenging aspect of the project, the developer says, was the budget. Research had shown that the typical new "main street" retail centers were in upscale markets, with boutique-style merchants paying high rents. White Marsh is solidly middle-market. The solution was found in creating a visual "main street" with a middle-market merchandise mix.

The result mixes contemporary flair and nostalgic concepts in an enjoyable locale for shopping, dining and entertainment. The Avenue includes a 16-screen cinema, six restaurants, children's educational retailers, a variety of specialty stores and entertainment-oriented retailers like music, video and book stores.

MAJOR TENANTS		
NAME	**TYPE**	**GLA (SQ. FT.)**
Loews Theaters	Multiscreen cinema	74,035
Barnes & Noble Booksellers	Bookstore	26,898
A. C. Moore	Crafts	24,000

Diagonal parking and a civic scale of design communicate The Avenue's "main street" presence.

A festive atmosphere grows from the abundant use of freestanding open-air kiosks, creative seating and paving patterns, and brilliantly colored graphics and signage. Street-side cafes, fountains, sculpture and lush landscaping add to the ambiance. The surrounding communities have embraced The Avenue at White Marsh as "their" community center. Holiday parades, school performances and benefit activities reinforce the mall's identity as a good neighbor.

Traditional "main street" design elements (opposite page) such as a movie theater and a "town square" fountain get contemporary design treatments.

Variety in rooftop shapes and heights (above) lend individuality to stores that were commonly planned.

The developer reports that providing adequate parking was an issue during the planning process. Most parking is at the rear of stores, with some diagonal parking along the "main street" itself.

One other issue was making "main street" walkable from a merchandising standpoint and in terms of distance alone. The centrally located theater building is about 420 feet long, which would have presented a long stretch of unbroken wall. The solution was to add six small blocks of space totaling 9,585 square feet to enliven the theater wall; these became the highest rent-per-square-foot spaces in the project.

In hindsight, the developer says the sidewalks along the "main street" might have been wider. A balance needed to be achieved between a wide-enough sidewalk and maintaining a civic-scale intimacy. Face-of-building to face-of-building distance is now 92 feet. The developer suggests the sidewalks might each be widened from 12 feet to 14 feet, adding 4 more feet to the overall street width.

Lively banners and turn-of-the-century-style street lamps exemplify how traditional concepts are mixed with modern design at The Avenue at White Marsh.

Design of an earlier period is suggested by the wrought-iron design of a mall directory (right), awnings and roof crown detail (below).

Over a short period of time, The Avenue at White Marsh has become a vital part of the White Marsh planned community and regional retailing. The developer credits the success to the design of the project, the "main street" orientation and the comfortable architecture. The increased demand for office space in the area has also been attributed to the center's presence.

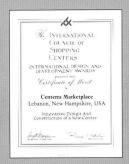

Owner:

Dartmouth College Real Estate Inc.

Hanover, New Hampshire, United States

Architect/Designer:

Arrowstreet Inc.

Somerville, Massachusetts, United States

Centerra Marketplace

Lebanon, New Hampshire, United States

Gross size of center:
59,585 sq. ft.

Gross leasable area excluding anchors:
59,585 sq. ft.

Total acreage of site:
10.7 acres

Type of center:
Neighborhood center

Physical description:
Strip center

Location of trading area:
Rural

Population:
- Primary trading area
  35,000
- Secondary trading area
  120,000
- Annualized percentage of shoppers
  anticipated to be from outside trade area
  35%

Development schedule:
- Original opening date
  October 1997

Parking spaces:
- Present number
  343

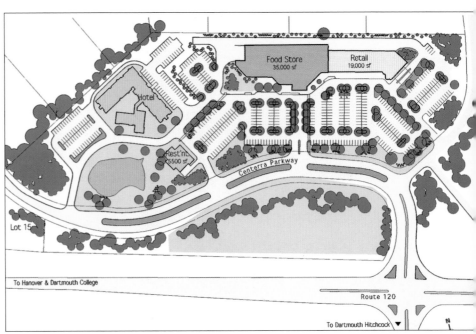

An aerial view of Centerra Marketplace (above) shows the forested entrance drive. The site plan (top right) shows how "green" a center and its environs can be. Elevation and section detail (below right) show the community scale of the project.

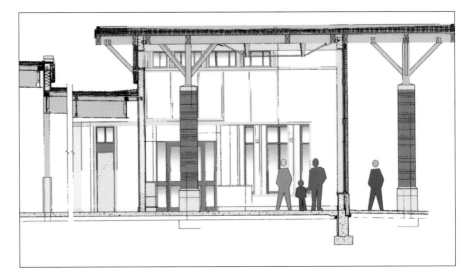

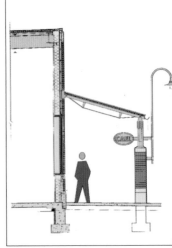

*C*enterra Marketplace is a new village shopping center in the midst of a business/industrial park. The developers wanted to energize the business park by providing a round-the-clock retail, dining and hospitality destination. The architects were challenged to create an intimate shopping center that would fit into the surrounding New England landscape, serve as a community gathering place and demonstrate the principles of environmentally conscious design.

In addition to a cooperative supermarket, the center includes an Asian-style bistro, a bank, and a boutique selling children's upscale merchandise and clothing. A Residence Inn is adjacent to the center.

Approaching the project from the main road, which is accessible via interstate to nearby Dartmouth College, the center evokes the image of a 19th-century New England farm village. Achieving this effect required non-typical strip center site planning. Mature trees around the center were preserved, the parking lot was broken up by small pods and the entry drive was gently curved.

The simple Shaker forms of wood, brick and steel are reflected in an octagonal bank building (above right) and the co-op food store (right).

*Covered sidewalks
are an integral
architectural element
of the center, and
echo the front
porches of New
England farmhouses.*

The building mass of wood, brick and metal is nestled against a backdrop of rolling hills. The center is topped by the Shaker-inspired octagonal cupola of the main tenant. Substantial covered walkways, echoing the front porches of farmhouses, modulate the mass of the building and offer shelter to patrons.

The developer wanted to use an environmentally conscious "green" design. Environmental goals were balanced with the owner's financial requirements. Materials had to prove aesthetically attractive and durable. New England Electric Systems provided economic incentives for energy-saving goals, which allowed the major tenants to investigate several interesting ways of cutting back on energy use. In some cases, new technologies were either unproven or cost-prohibitive, which led to the exploration of techniques for reengineering standard technologies for greater efficiencies.

The food store exterior (below) and its interior (left) carry through simple design elements of an earlier era.

In the food store, sensors read levels of daylight through the food co-op skylights and adjust electric lighting accordingly.

MAJOR TENANT

NAME	TYPE	GLA (SQ. FT.)
Lebanon Co-Op Food Store	Supermarket	35,231

The most significant energy-saving component in the Co-Op Food Store is the skylights. Sensors in the market detect the level of light and adjust electric lighting accordingly. It is anticipated that the market will save $55,000 a year in energy costs as compared to a typical grocery store.

Recycled or environmentally benign materials were used where possible, including recycled wood in the trusses, fly ash in the concrete and wastepaper in the countertops. Other products with recycled content are steel studs, vapor barriers, resilient flooring and tiles. The building's exterior is water-struck brick, a vernacular material of the region.

The centerpiece skylight in the food co-op is modeled on a Shaker-inspired octagon.

The restaurant's form and its sliding doors to the patio were inspired by local barn structures.

Centerra Marketplace shows how an environmentally conscious design can benefit both developer and customer, as well as how "green" design can be economically wise by saving energy costs. Centerra Marketplace achieves all this while providing a needed retail center and community gathering place for Lebanon and Hanover.

Owner:

Glendale Marketplace, LLC
Beverly Hills, California, United States

Architect/Designer:

Feola, Carli & Archuleta
Glendale, California, United States

Glendale Marketplace
Glendale, California, United States

Gross size of center:
163,889 sq. ft.

Gross leasable area excluding anchors:
32,155 sq. ft.

Total acreage of site:
2.22 acres

Type of center:
Theme/Festival community center

Physical description:
Open two-level mall

Location of trading area:
Suburban/Urban Central Business District

Population:
- Primary trading area
  207,984
- Secondary trading area
  560,756
- Annualized percentage of shoppers
  anticipated to be from outside trade area
  5%

Development schedule:
- Original opening date
  June 1, 1998

Parking spaces:
- Present number
  1,124

Innovative Design and Construction of a New Project

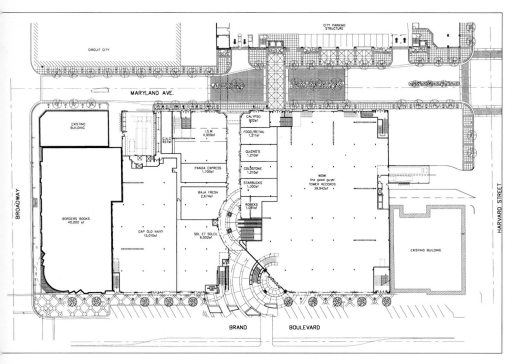

The lower-level lease plan (left) shows the importance of street access to Glendale Marketplace (below).

Glendale Marketplace is an urban village shopping center, a multilevel lifestyle center in the Los Angeles megalopolis. With a distinctive outdoor-oriented design reminiscent of a small Mediterranean village, Glendale Marketplace is unlike traditional malls in that it does not rely on anchors, such as department stores. Rather, its shopper draw comes from a strategic combination of tenants with powerful synergy, including a multiscreen theater, both high-turnover and "white tablecloth" restaurants, and major national lifestyle retailers.

Gardens create a community gathering place (above right). A young family enters the pedestrian paseo and outdoor dining area (right).

The theater and music/electronic retailers add to the entertainment focus of Glendale.

MAJOR TENANTS		
NAME	**TYPE**	**GLA (SQ. FT.)**
Linens 'n' Things	Home furnishings	41,018
Mann Theatres	Multiscreen cinema	35,764
Good Guys	Electronics	31,263
Old Navy	Clothing	15,010
Tower Records	Music	8,679

The center occupies a constrained urban site, and management of the design process was complicated, requiring the coordination of often-conflicting requirements of tenants and a redevelopment authority's architectural consultant. Proximity of stores created other issues, such as sound leakage from the theaters and a record store, which were solved through the use of sound-absorbing detailing of the structural connections. Yet another problem was a seven-foot slope on what was supposedly a flat urban parcel; careful relocation of a paseo avoided any step-down at the storefronts.

The natural tones of the Southwest (above) change to lively light at night (right).

The village concept is borne out in this view (left) from the second-level pedestrian walkway into the paseo. Below, classical columns blend with a brightly lit sign at a juice store.

Public-private partnership dealt with some key issues. City government agreed to subsidize the land cost and pay for the construction of a multilevel parking deck that connects to the Marketplace's second floor. The developer completed the assembly of the land (12 parcels under separate ownership) and all development costs. The developer also met with relevant community groups, businesses and homeowner groups to involve them all in the design process. The sense of community involvement was enhanced by the developer raising $75,000 for a local neonatal intensive care unit.

A movie theater complex attracts visitors with its lively entrance (above). An escalator takes shoppers from the cinema box office to the second-level tenants (right). A storefront reflects the Southwestern theme (bottom).

Glendale Marketplace's fountain is especially designed for kids with its whimsical climbing frogs.

In terms of design, Glendale Marketplace plays off Southern California's Spanish heritage. Internal outdoor streets called paseos link the project to the Glendale urban fabric. The main entrance is marked by a custom-designed fountain of three larger-than-life frogs spewing steams of water, under which children are welcome to play. A festive rotunda is the centerpiece for ongoing entertainment events and a Kids Club. Careful store placement allows adequate mall area, despite the tight site.

Even though most tenants were deemed to be strong credits by lenders and appealed to the lifestyle and demographic groups in the trade area, none had previous presence in the market. The mix proved so successful that each of the major stores voluntarily extended its operating hours late into the evening, resulting in sales figures considerably beyond expectations. Parking validations show that most visitors stay longer than two hours, indicating that the mix of retail and entertainment works well at Glendale Marketplace.

Photos: Ronald Moore Photography

Owner:

The Rubin Jefferson Partnership

Los Angeles, California, United States

Architect/Designer:

MCG Architecture

Pasadena, California, United States

Main Place

Naperville, Illinois, United States

Gross size of center:
73,363 sq. ft.

Gross leasable area excluding anchors:
44,634 sq. ft.

Total acreage of site:
1.68 acres

Type of center:
Neighborhood center

Physical description:
Open mixed-use mall

Location of trading area:
Suburban main street

Population:
- Primary trading area
  120,000
- Secondary trading area
  200,546
- Annualized percentage of shoppers anticipated to be from outside trade area
  40%

Development schedule:
- Original opening date
  November 28, 1997

Parking spaces:
- Present number
  72

Diagonal street parking is reminiscent of midcentury America.

*M*ain Place in downtown Naperville, Illinois, combines retail, office and residential elements in a Modern Federalist-style building using traditional brick facade and decorative stone detailing.

The developer sought to create the feeling of a town square at the turn of the century. The two-story design of Main Place respects the scale of Naperville's historic core, which averages one to three stories. Second-story apartments allow shopkeepers and others to reside above the stores in the manner of a traditional downtown. The second-story spaces have a separate access point on a side street, allowing privacy and avoiding conflict with retail street traffic.

The "main street" appearance is reinforced by the location of most parking at the rear of the project. A limited amount of diagonal street parking, as would be found in older downtowns, is located in front of the project.

MAJOR TENANTS

NAME	TYPE	GLA (SQ. FT.)
Eddie Bauer	Outdoor/Apparel	19,000
Talbot's and Talbot's Petites	Apparel	8,330
Ann Taylor and Ann Taylor Shoes	Apparel/Shoes	4,150
Wolf Camera and Video	Camera store	1,361

Main Place's retailers get high visibility in harmony with the historical design concept.

The brick facades and ornate street lamp fixtures remind shoppers of earlier times.

The period design is enhanced by brick-paved pedestrian walkways, which lead from the rear parking area to Naperville's River Walk. The walkway was structured to allow city crews access to a 48 inch storm sewer pipe below the walkway. A pedestrian breezeway reaffirms the civic scale of the project and becomes a unifying link between the building and the neighborhood.

Walkways tie the project to the surrounding neighborhood.

Store sales benefit from display windows (above) at curbside. Terracotta design elements (right) lend simplicity to modern retailing.

Ornate passages between the buildings host the center's signage and unify the stores' presence. Corner clock towers anchor the project. An issue with a subdivision law was solved by installing ornamental barrel archways with the project name at both ends of a pedestrian breezeway, thus making the project a single building.

Retailers enjoy prominent curbside windows, encouraging shoppers to enter from the street. Stores get greater identity from the building's tall and articulated facade, signage and tall towers.

Ornamental barrel archways define the project boundaries.

*Main Place provides
an atmosphere that
conveys both a
downtown and a
shopping center
feeling.*

This new upscale neighborhood
shopping center has jump-started
Naperville's central business
district, increasing foot traffic for
other retailers and restaurants, as
well as contributing to sales and
property taxes.

The developer sees the project as
an example of continuing trends:
establishing a "main street" in
suburban areas and further
diversification of shopping
locations. Main Place does so by
surrounding new retailers with
old world charm.

Certificate of Merit

Owner:

The Prudential Assurance Co. Ltd. and JT Baylis & Co. Ltd.

London, United Kingdom

Architect/Designer:

Building Design Partnership

London, United Kingdom

The Mall, Cribbs Causeway

Bristol, United Kingdom

Gross size of center:
725,000 sq. ft.

Gross leasable area excluding anchors:
350,000 sq. ft.

Total acreage of site:
70 acres

Type of center:
Regional fashion/Specialty center

Physical description:
Two-level enclosed mall

Location of trading area:
Suburban/Rural

Population:
- Primary trading area
  1,700,000
- Secondary trading area
  1,700,000

Development schedule:
- Original opening date
  March 31, 1998

Parking spaces:
- Present number
  7,000

Photo: Roger Ball

A water feature and twin rows of trees point the way to The Mall, Cribbs Causeway.

The Mall, Cribbs Causeway, is a two-level enclosed regional mall in a semi-rural area near Bristol in southwest England. The design and development team sought to produce a center that would combine optimal commercial efficiency with timeless architecture.

A rigorous period of design analysis identified the need for a mall with maximum tenant visibility, one where all the shops on both levels would have equal value and the pedestrian flow would be balanced. Anchors would need to be visible from the mall's center. Further, the team wanted maximum flexibility of shop layout and a design that would not soon become outdated.

Photo: Charlotte Wood

Landscaped grounds (above) are a valued amenity for shoppers, who are attracted (below) to high-visibility tenants.

Photo: Roger Ball

A huge atrium lets in the maximum available sunlight.

Photo: Roger Ball

The result was a virtually column-free mall containing elegant shallow pilasters and glass balustrades. There is ample visibility between the levels and along the mall length. Escalators, carefully positioned in the angles of two changes in mall direction, do not block views of the anchor stores.

Public spaces are meant as a neutral setting for the shops and use high-quality, durable and easily maintained materials. A continuous glazed roof with solar shades creates dappled sunlight in the summer and architectural enclosure when floodlit at night. In all, the developer says, the design is achieved without recourse to any stylistic panache and is truly modern in nature.

Photo: David Barbour

Left: A fountain, wide sidewalks and rows of trees offer a friendly welcome. Escalators (below) were placed so as not to block the views of anchor stores.

Photo: Roger Ball

Left: Palms do well under the natural skylight. Above: A store directory shows simple store layout.

Photos: David Barbour

MAJOR TENANTS

NAME	TYPE	GLA (SQ. FT.)
John Lewis Partnership	Department store	230,000
Marks & Spencer	Fashion stores	146,000

Technically, the mall is unique in the United Kingdom for its displacement air ventilation system, which provides clean air for the building via the shopfront pilasters and extracts dirty warm air at high levels. Artificial lighting provides a soft ambiance meant not to distract from store displays. In the Focal Court, special computer-controlled lights project stunning patterns on the roof during the winter. At the heart of the center is a multi-jet computer-controlled fountain.

Landscaping — informal around the perimeter with lines of trees on the axis of the main entrances — culminates in a central grand avenue of twin rows of trees on either side of lawns and fountains, stretching from the site entrance to the Food Court glass wall.

Storefronts maximize opportunities for merchandise display. Below left: The Mall, Cribbs Causeway, is almost column-free.

Photos: Charlotte Wood

A fountain serves as a gathering point within the vast scale of the center (left). The glazed roof is floodlit at night, creating a dramatic view for visitors (below).

Photo: Roger Ball

The developer says the center is successful for several key reasons: the mall's proximity to major roadways, public transportation (which brings 20 percent of customers), ample free parking and the clarity of the layout. Further, a hands-on approach to management coupled with rent agreements created a common positive attitude. All consultants, the main contractor and the developer were housed in one office during the design and construction period, contributing greatly to a smoothly run project and the ultimate success of The Mall, Cribbs Causeway.

Photo: Charlotte Wood

Owner:
Viejas Tribal Council
Alpine, California, United States

Architect:
Sollberg + Lowe
Marina Del Rey, California, United States

Designer:
Bullock, Smith & Partners
Knoxville, Tennessee, United States

Viejas Outlet Center
Alpine, California, United States

Gross size of center:
187,000 sq. ft.

Gross leasable area excluding anchors:
174,496 sq. ft.

Total acreage of site:
50 acres

Type of center:
Outlet center

Physical description:
Village

Location of trading area:
Suburban

Population:
- Primary trading area
  1,700,000
- Secondary trading area
  1,000,000
- Annualized percentage of shoppers
  anticipated to be from outside trade area
  25%

Development schedule:
- Original opening date
  May 22, 1998
- Future expansion
  Spring 2000

Parking spaces:
- Present number
  940

The main court of Viejas Outlet Center unmistakably communicates a Native American heritage.

Viejas Outlet Center is an upscale value retail center on the Viejas Indian reservation adjacent to the Viejas Casino and Turf Club. The center's 38 tenants are clustered in a village of eight retail structures connected by intimate passages, which circulate through six courtyards that serve as focal points and contain ceremonial features. The center Show Court is the heart of the project and offers entertainment nightly.

The Show Court
(above) entertains
shoppers at night.
The site plan (below)
shows major
buildings and the
various plazas —
a Fire Court, an Air
Court, a Water Court
and an Earth Court.

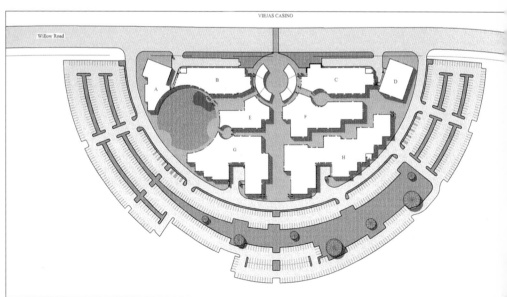

A sparse Western setting at one of the courts (top). An open green space (above) attracts families seeking a break from shopping.

More than 24 million tourists visit the area annually — they became a target market. Economic consultants estimate that the center alone will draw 2 million visitors per year.

The Viejas Tribal Council wanted a design that reflected their Native American heritage and integrated the natural surroundings. The current Viejas residents are descended from the Kumeyaay Indians, who have sheltered themselves minimally in the temperate climate of California and who lack a distinguishable architectural style.

Designers began with a base of Southwestern lines and colors, adding twisting branches, stones and other natural materials to create a unique style. The team developed a series of symbols, based in part on Kumeyaay hieroglyphics, to represent the natural themes of the complex. Contemporary elements were added in the form of technological aspects, colors, graphics and clean building lines.

The open-air design of the center offers views of Alpine's dramatic cloud formations and nearby mountains. Designers worked around the site's natural vegetation and used on-site natural borders when laying out the project. Rock formations, water features and plant life characteristic of Alpine's river valley pepper the walkways and courtyards.

Stone outcroppings (left) define walkways, attracting pedestrians to stores. A project storefront blends neatly into the natural palette of the center (below).

A view from the center to the adjacent casino and the mountains beyond.

The chilly mist of London fog is nowhere to be seen at this desert-themed storefront. Opposite page: Rustic design (top) blends with the swoosh. Water features entertain at the Show Court during the day (right).

MAJOR TENANTS

NAME	TYPE	GLA (SQ. FT.)
Nike Outlet	Value retail store	14,485
Liz Claiborne Outlet	Value retail store	11,900
Linen Barn	Value retail store	11,300
Gap Outlet	Value retail store	11,260

The village's circular layout pays tribute to the Native American symbol of the medicine wheel, and its illumination at night attracts the attention of airline passengers flying into the nearby San Diego airport.

The Show Court, which offers a live-action show each night, re-creates a ceremonial ground where elders told stories around the fire; the developer would enlarge the Show Court's capacity, given the chance. Directly across the street from the casino, the Show Court entertains guests after the shopping day ends and lets them rest before moving into the casino.

Viejas Outlet Center has enhanced the attraction of the Viejas Casino and Turf Club, with casino revenue increasing since the shopping village opened.

Viejas Outlet Center demonstrates how an outlet center can successfully escape typical strip development by creating a unique contextual concept.

A deer sculpture (left) reminds shoppers of local wildlife. The Show Court is shaded part of the day (below).

Certificate of Merit

Owner:

Mitsui Fudosan Co. Ltd.
Yokohama, Kanagawa-Ken, Japan

Architect:

Mitsui Construction Co. Ltd.
Yokohama, Kanagawa-Ken, Japan

Designer:

RTKL Associates Inc.
Baltimore, Maryland, United States

Yokohama Bayside Marina Shops and Restaurants
Yokohama, Kanagawa-Ken, Japan

Gross size of center:
208,518 sq. ft.

Gross leasable area excluding anchors:
175,678 sq. ft.

Total acreage of site:
7.9 acres

Type of center:
Theme/Festival outlet center

Physical description:
Open two-level mall

Location of trading area:
Waterfront

Population:
- Primary trading area
  7.5 million
- Secondary trading area
  10 - 15 million
- Annualized percentage of shoppers
  anticipated to be from outside trade area
  20%

Development schedule:
- Original opening date
  March 2, 1998

Parking spaces:
- Present number
  1,200

Innovative Design and Construction of a New Project

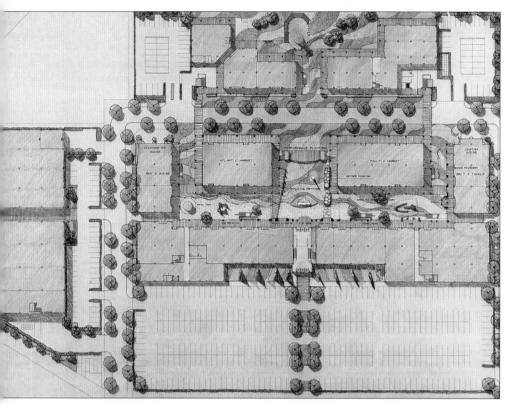

The site plan and
aerial view of
Yokohama Bayside
Marina Shops show
its proximity to the
waterfront.

A short-term land-lease agreement with the City of Yokohama meant that a project on the site would have a 10-year life expectancy, after which more permanent development could be slated. The result — Yokohama Bayside Marina Shops and Restaurants — is a low-cost, high-impact retail/entertainment project that combines 50 outlet stores with nine themed restaurants and a supermarket.

The theme of a New England fishing village is evident everywhere in the project.

The project blends
new and international
retailers with
playground amenities.
Opposite page:
Weathervanes and a
windmill dominate
the skyline of the
project.

MAJOR TENANTS

NAME	TYPE	GLA (SQ. FT.)
Nike	Sporting goods	10,415
Mont Bell	Outdoor/Casual	8,180
World	Women's apparel	5,121

The owner wanted to capitalize on Yokohama's historical status as Japan's chief seaport and envisioned the development as a picturesque New England fishing village. An accompanying story line tells the tale of a boy and a group of fishermen aboard a whaling ship from Nantucket. The ship follows whales for weeks and becomes lost at sea. The boy befriends a whale calf that leads the ship and its crew to a new home, where the fishermen construct a new town in the likeness of their New England village home.

The nautical theme appears in store directories and signage.

Historic images of signs, building types and letter styles were thoroughly researched to authenticate the design of the buildings. The resulting project captures the quaintness of a Nantucket waterside hamlet with small shops, traditional building forms, theme-insired spaces, a pedestrian promenade and a central lighthouse. Many of the buildings are topped with weathervanes, painted to mimic the patina of a weathered copper vane. Shoppers regularly look past nautical-inspired graphics to see the waterfront beyond, blending art and nature in a retail environment.

Even in store signs, Yokohama Bayside Marina Shops ties into the waterfront motif.

The needs of retailers were paramount in overall planning. For example, colors of the buildings were chosen from a pale palette and appear aged, so as not to compete visually with tenant graphics, which were likely to be brightly colored. Restaurant tenant graphics were created by the designer and carried through by the eateries' staffs in the shirts, hats and other apparel they wear at work.

The idea of a waterfront as a lifestyle amenity is emerging in Japan. Yokohama Bayside Marina Shops occupies what used to be an industrial location and serves as an anchor for urban redevelopment. The project also played an important role in bringing eight new retailers to Japan. Not only is it Japan's largest outlet center, but the developers say that this American streetscape offers an enjoyable escape from Japanese daily life.

Precise attention to detail makes it possible to introduce Western ideas into Eastern culture at Yokohama Bayside Marina Shops and Restaurants.

Owner:
Old Mutual Properties
Cape Town, South Africa

Architect/Designer:
Development Design Group, Inc.
Baltimore, Maryland, United States

Cavendish Square
Claremont, Cape Town,
South Africa

Gross size of center:
429,523 sq. ft.

Gross leasable area excluding anchors:
221,607 sq. ft.

Total acreage of site:
5.8 acres

Type of center:
Regional center

Physical description:
Enclosed mall

Location of trading area:
Urban but not downtown

Population:
- Primary trading area
  150,000
- Secondary trading area
  150,000
- Annualized percentage of shoppers
  anticipated to be from outside trade area
  fewer than 1%

Development schedule:
- Original opening date
  October 1973
- Current expansion date
  May 1998
- Future expansion
  Spring 2000

Parking spaces:
- Present number
  1,850
- 750 parking spaces added in renovation

Located near the Cape Town shore, Cavendish Square's entrance changed from sparse to dazzling.

*R*enovation and expansion of Cavendish Square in Cape Town, South Africa, demonstrates how thinking "outside the box" can produce excellent results.

A 25-year-old enclosed regional mall, Cavendish Square was outdated architecturally and in tenant mix. Beyond the burdens of a "concrete fortress" exterior, significant market changes, increased competition, obsolete mechanical, electrical and seismic provisions, a nearly one-fifth vacancy rate and ill-configured parking, the owners sought a design solution and international tenant mix.

"Major reconstructive surgery" was how the developer portrayed the project, which would not expand the center's footprint. Mechanical, electrical and seismic systems were renewed to meet or exceed international codes. Columns were strengthened to accept three rooftop parking levels. A new third shopping level was added, expanding retail space by 37 percent.

MAJOR TENANTS

NAME	TYPE	GLA (SQ. FT.)
Stuttaford's	Department store	107,682
Ster Kinekor Cineplex	Multiscreen cinema	57,049
Exclusive Books	Bookstore	4,951

A new speed ramp (right) improves flow and removes traffic from neighboring streets.

A dramatic new skylight entrance and new floor openings bring light into the center court from seven levels above and emphasizes vertical movement, bringing shoppers to the upper levels. Vertical transportation was reconfigured, including the addition of two new full-size scenic elevators. The rooftop level entrance welcomes shoppers with a lush "garden in the sky." Access to rooftop parking was eased through a new vehicular speed ramp, ending traffic backups on surrounding streets. Sleek escalators replaced dark stairwells.

Thirty new international tenants were added, including globally known names such as Levi's, Timberland, ACA Joe, Swatch and McDonald's. People seeking entertainment and food frequent a 16-screen cinema (South Africa's largest multiplex), a music megastore, 10 new restaurants and a cafe court.

Graphic changes tied closely to retail and entertainment goals. New shop windows and showcases were created at street level, where structurally possible around the building's exterior, attracting passersby. Large illuminated advertising panels were installed. The center's visual impact was enhanced by the expansive center court atrium, interior design, more open vertical access points and new graphics.

Shapes, light and movement attract shoppers' eyes upward to higher levels of retail.

Dreary mall areas (left) were replaced by lively expanses of glass, tile and light (below and opposite).

The center remained open throughout the massive construction. Work continued 24 hours per day, with the most obtrusive construction avoiding regular shopping hours. Many tenants were temporarily relocated; guides in the malls assisted customers with finding their way. Full-time safety officers were employed for the entire construction period. Parking during construction was eased by hiring more attendants and a valet service via golf carts to move customers from cars to the elevators.

Cavendish Square completely changed its identity, inside and out, bringing global retailing to a once-outdated center.

Even store directories (below) have an artistic touch.

Storefronts are energized by bringing merchandise into better view.

Owner:
Equitable Asset Management
New York, New York, United States

Architect/Designer:
Altoon + Porter Architects
Los Angeles, California, United States

Fashion Valley Center

San Diego, California, United States

Gross size of center:
1,721,481 sq. ft.

Gross leasable area excluding anchors:
668,176 sq. ft.

Total acreage of site:
82.5 acres

Type of center:
Super-regional center

Physical description:
Open mall

Location of trading area:
Urban but not downtown

Population:
- Primary trading area
  1,077,701
- Secondary trading area
  492,341
- Annualized percentage of shoppers anticipated to be from outside trade area 30%

Development schedule:
- Original opening date
  Fall 1969
- Current expansion date
  Fall 1997

Parking spaces:
- Present number
  8,894
- 3,704 parking spaces added in renovation

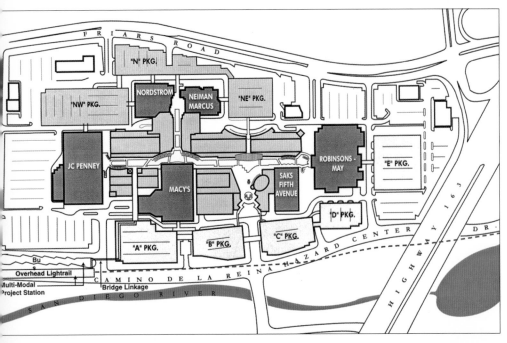

*E*nvironmental issues and a restricted site are just two of the reasons why developers chose both vertical and horizontal expansion in renovating the nearly 30-year-old Fashion Valley Shopping Center.

The site plan (left) shows direct access from parking decks to second-level retailers at Fashion Valley Center. Below, diners in the food court see the nighttime sky behind the main mall entry.

Pairs of palms lend elegance to the new mall entry at night.

The center sits in a valley bounded by roads and a freeway to the north and east, and to the south by the San Diego River, whose floodplain has critical mandates from the U.S. Army Corps of Engineers. An overhead light rail line and bus station were proposed to run on the property's south side. Plans for the new second level were further complicated by the need to create an independent structural system, since the site is subject to soil liquefaction when serious earthquakes strike.

Creating retail "precincts" presented a solution to many of these problems. Multiple elevation changes, needed to serve the department store entries, provided the opportunity to bring the center's large size down to a smaller scale. Each precinct was designed to be characteristically different from the others. Throughout the center, a "Main Street" sense of community was achieved through the use of civic-scaled design, incorporating terraces, colonnades and trellised walkways.

The tenant mix was significantly reconfigured, bringing in new retailers unique to the area. Food and beverage selection was expanded through a new food court terrace. An 18-screen cinema extends the center's activity well into the night, and linkage to the new light rail system brings in customers from adjoining urban centers.

Use of a "dancing trellis" (above) and the view from a pedestrian bridge (left) demonstrate how space can be defined without sacrificing the view of the sky.

A storefront bathed in natural light (right) shows the civic scale of the project.

MAJOR TENANTS		
NAME	**TYPE**	**GLA (SQ. FT.)**
JC Penney	Department store	253,212
Nordstrom	Department store	220,486
Macy's	Department store	196,120
Robinsons-May	Department store	171,625
Neiman Marcus	Department store	105,144
Saks Fifth Avenue	Department store	80,000
AMC	Multiscreen cinema	20,715

Each of the mall levels has been artfully designed.

No surface, whether graphics or parking entrances, was left untouched by design elements.

The center remained open for the entire redevelopment period. The architect's experience with four other vertical expansion projects helped reduce inconvenience to shoppers during construction. Shopper safety was of primary concern. When possible, construction was done at night or prior to mall operating hours. Scaffolding was erected to allow construction during the day. Graphics told shoppers "Rome wasn't built in a day" and featured pictures of the grand landmarks in architectural history.

A cross-mall view (above) demonstrates how development and nature can blend. Even fixtures (above left) are tied into the trellis design theme.

Easy public access brings shoppers to the greater shopping experiences at the renovated and expanded Fashion Valley Center.

A special challenge for the leasing team was convincing some tenants to relocate to the second level after the build-out. The quality of the space and the convenient pool of parking at that level convinced many to accept the offer. The developer reports that second-level sales outperform that of the lower level.

Beyond better service to local customers, the center now attracts 15% more shoppers from other countries than before. Mission Valley's renovation and expansion shows that an imaginative approach to environmental issues can enhance a project's appeal to the shopper.

Photos: Erhard Pfeiffer

Owner:

Banmak Associates

King of Prussia, Pennsylvania, United States

Architect/Designer:

Arrowstreet Inc.

Somerville, Massachusetts, United States

Bangor Mall

Bangor, Maine, United States

Gross size of center:
490,557 sq. ft.

Amount of space renovated:
160,715 sq. ft.

Total acreage of site:
94 acres

Type of center:
Super-regional center

Physical description:
Enclosed one-level mall

Location of trading area:
Middle market

Population:
- Primary trading area
  128,000
- Secondary trading area
  143,000
- Annualized percentage of shoppers
  anticipated to be from outside trade area
  25%

Development schedule:
- Original opening date
  October 5, 1978
- Current expansion date
  November 12, 1997
- Future expansion
  November 12, 1998

Parking spaces:
- Present number
  3,536

Before-and-after photos of a typical mall entrance show how the entry now stands out from the facade.

At 20 years old, the Bangor Mall needed an image upgrade to remain competitive and generate new business. The mall reflected the design values of the late 1970s and had not aged well. Both its exterior and interior were dated and dark. The color scheme of the arcade floor (bland brown-and-yellow quarry tile) and dark wood wall finishes gave off a somber feeling. The darkness was exacerbated by low light levels dictated by a restrictive energy code and the original desire to make retailers stand out by keeping the arcade itself dim. The arcade was cluttered by many built-in planters, seating areas and fountains, which obstructed sightlines and blocked customer circulation. Outside, the center's signage was dated and entrances did not stand out from the facade.

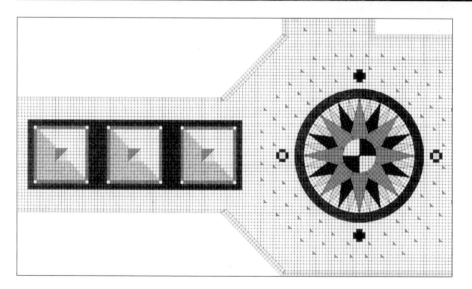

Tile patterns reflect the Maine setting (clockwise from upper left): log cabin, mariners' compass, pine tree, and pine cones and needles.

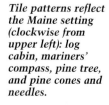

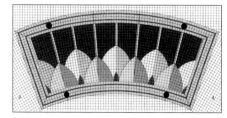

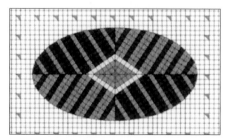

The JC Penney court was renovated with an enlarged skylight, marble tile and an unobstructed view of the anchor store.

Center court before was cluttered and dark. After renovation, light and space abound.

MAJOR TENANTS

NAME	TYPE	GLA (SQ. FT.)
Sears	Department store	105,817
JC Penney	Department store	95,082
Porteous	Department store	68,052
Doug's Shop & Save	Grocery store	40,080

A flat market and little population growth in this area of Maine meant that growth would not occur within the mall's primary trade area, so the developer sought to increase sales by expanding the mall's catchment area. This would be achieved by strengthening tenant mix with nationally recognized tenants and creating elegant interiors.

Architects targeted the floors, ceiling, skylights and lighting to rejuvenate the mall. Existing skylights of varied sizes and shapes were replaced with large skylights of a unified shape. Custom pendant uplights now echo the outlines of floor patterns. Designers created a new curved skylight to link the legs of the mall and visually expand the center court. These decisions improved the sense of space and the amount of natural light coming into the mall.

The former arcade (below right) was bland and dated. A renovated intermediate court (below left) benefits from enlarged skylights, oval ceiling coffers, tile patterns and new lighting. Honeycomb light fixtures (bottom right) were replaced by a curving skylight (bottom left).

The marble floors are the most dramatic element of the renovation. The entire floor of quarry tile was covered with high-honed marble tile of mostly cream and light colors in traditional American quilt patterns. The designers recast the mall's arcade in pale, muted colors. A design theme relates the interior to the northern Maine woods. At center court, the designers sheathed four existing structural columns in white and added two matching decorative columns for symmetry. They created illuminated column capitals in a snowflake design from laser-cut aluminum. A skylight added to center court was the only structural change in the entire renovation.

A storefront, once surrounded by dull, muted tones, now beckons shoppers (opposite page) with light, a column and plantings.

A lighter, more up-to-date atmosphere in the mall's public areas is a welcome change.

Designers of Bangor Mall achieved their goals with a new look in the floors, ceiling, skylight and lighting.

The mall was kept open during the renovation, but most work was done after shopping hours. Barricades provided shopper safety and organized traffic flow during daytime construction. The various construction disciplines were closely coordinated. For example, work on ceilings was timed to coincide with work on the floor directly underneath, through the use of over-under scaffolding.

Beyond new nationally recognized tenants such as The Disney Store, The Gap and The Children's Place, several amenities were added: cushioned benches, lockers, a winter coat check service, an expanded food court and oversize restroom facilities that included family restrooms and nursing rooms. A new logo incorporating the image of indigenous pine completed the renovation of Bangor Mall.

International Council of Shopping Centers
23rd International Design and Development Awards

Certificate of Merit

Owner:

The Rouse Company

Columbia, Maryland,
United States

Architect/Designer:

RTKL Associates Inc.

Dallas, Texas, United States

Beachwood Place

Beachwood, Ohio, United States

Gross size of center:
918,000 sq. ft.

Gross leasable area excluding anchors:
354,000 sq. ft.

Total acreage of site:
60 acres

Type of center:
Super-regional center

Physical description:
Enclosed mall

Location of trading area:
Suburban

Population:
- Primary trading area
  200,000

- Secondary trading area
  110,000

- Annualized percentage of shoppers
  anticipated to be from outside trade area
  20%

Development schedule:
- Original opening date
  1977

- Current expansion date
  September 1997

Parking spaces:
- Present number
  4,000

*L*ocated in an affluent Cleveland suburb, Beachwood Place was a "jewel box" when it opened in 1979 — intimately scaled retail pavilions. While well maintained and attractive, 18 years later the mall's design and details had become dated. Sales were strong, but the flourishing suburbs held even greater sales potential if the mall were renovated and attracted new retailers.

The mall's entrance was revitalized with a streetscape, including merchandise displays and storefronts flanking a courtyard. A new Eddie Bauer Premiere store was given anchor prominence next to the new entry; its contemporary steel-and-glass towers fit into the original design. The main entry tower is clad in natural slate, which glows at night like a lantern, with light spilling from the glass at its upturned roof.

On the interior, the expansion deliberately re-created the same volumes of space as in the original design, with wood screens lining pitched roofs and skylights. In both the expansion and the renovated sections, new design ideas were introduced. A French limestone floor was placed in the interior concourses. Contemporary furniture groupings were flanked by screens of French flower buckets to add a residential ambiance.

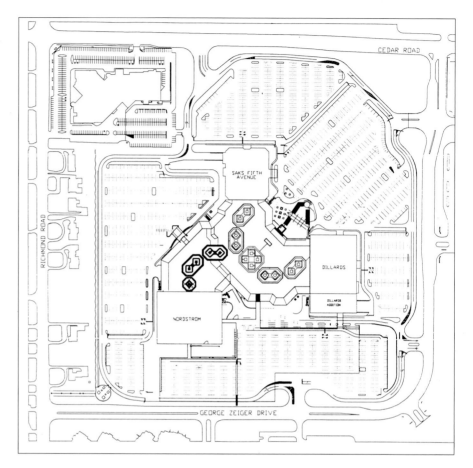

The site plan for Beachwood Place shows the prominent location of the new Nordstrom store.

Opposite page: The renovation featured towers and outdoor walkways (top and far right) to give a more open feeling to the exterior, which had become outdated (near right).

MAJOR TENANTS

NAME	TYPE	GLA (SQ. FT.)
Nordstrom	Department store	250,000
Dillard's	Department store	247,000
Eddie Bauer Premiere	Outdoor/Apparel	30,000

Instead of typical fountains that would need to be covered for an event or performance, Beachwood Place offers fountains with backlit glass platforms that hover over the water and double as runways for fashion shows and displays. Backlit fabric "lampshade" canopies line the ceilings of the entrances. Light woods are used as accents in handrails and furniture. Soft colors were used on painted column and wall surfaces, with white, ochre and sage greens used to differentiate each wing of the mall.

The food court was reduced in size to five tenants and treated like a small cafe, with a higher level of finish and lighting than is found in most food courts. The upscale cafe concept is carried through in suspended lanterns and paneled wood ceilings and signs.

The addition of a Nordstrom department store attracted other upscale retailers new to the Cleveland area: Pottery Barn, Guess and a new retail concept called the Galleries of Neiman Marcus, in addition to the Eddie Bauer Premiere store. In all, over 50 new shops and three upscale restaurants were brought in.

With Beachwood Place's loyal customer base (five visits per month), it was crucial to maintain the center's intimate and human-scale ambiance while upgrading finishes and tenants. Most construction was done at night, with extensive efforts by the contractor to screen construction areas during the day.

The use of glass, steel and stone offers an upscale appeal.

Inside Beachwood Place, the old dark storefronts and floor (below) gave way to lighter hues (right).

The developer credits close cooperation with the design team as important to the success of the renovation/expansion. The new components of flooring, more color, lighting and furniture, plus the new tenant mix enhanced rather than changed the quality of Beachwood shopping.

A cluttered old view (right) was transformed with white, ochre and sage flooring and comfortable furnishings (below).

High fashion is on display even in the food court of Beachwood Place (right) and in a central fountain (below).

Patterns in skylights and walls show the power of understatement in design at the new Beachwood Place.

Certificate of Merit

Owner:

The Canada Life Assurance Company

Toronto, Ontario, Canada

Architect:

Ty Miller, Architect

Marina del Rey, California, United States

Designer:

Chase Parker Corporation

Santa Ana, California, United States

The Manteca Marketplace
Manteca, California, United States

Gross size of center:
174,779 sq. ft.

Gross leasable area excluding anchors:
43,870 sq. ft.

Total acreage of site:
13 acres

Type of center:
Neighborhood/Community center

Physical description:
Strip center

Location of trading area:
Suburban

Population:
- Primary trading area
  54,320
- Secondary trading area
  65,093
- Annualized percentage of shoppers anticipated to be from outside trade area
  1%

Development schedule:
- Original opening date
  1972

Parking spaces:
- Present number
  759
- 47 parking spaces added in renovation

The vacant Kmart store (above) was transformed into a 10-plex, all-stadium cinema (right) that became the focal point of The Manteca Marketplace.

*T*he owner of what is now The Manteca Marketplace had taken the shopping center back through foreclosure. The then-unnamed and dilapidated strip center was 58 percent vacant, and sales were declining among the tenants who remained. The old center was built in two phases (1972 and 1988), linked by a vacant Kmart department store and a common parking lot.

The location, however, convinced the owner that renovation and re-tenanting could prove productive. The developer called for a new image conveying quality, drama and entertainment that could be implemented economically while the center remained open and operational.

The renovation included replacing existing parking lot trees with contemporary lines of towering palm trees.

Neon and high-gloss tiles accent the new Stadium 10 lobby and concession area (above).

The former Kmart garden center (above) became an outdoor dining patio alongside the cinema (right).

Renovation or Expansion of an Existing Project

Bland storefronts (above and below) became glowing visual magnets, attracting shoppers at night (right).

By day, the large icon-based signage gives stores individual identities.

MAJOR TENANTS

NAME	TYPE	GLA (SQ. FT.)
Stadium 10	Multiscreen cinema	40,222
Save Mart	Supermarket	34,860
Rite Aid	Pharmacy	21,400

New architectural facades were designed for all existing buildings, layering simple three-dimensional forms on a common gridded wall. Towers, arcades and porticos were used for a signage program, controlled and subsidized by the developer, which required anchors to display their identities using colorful, oversized icons. Impressed by the signage, the city permitted four major pylon signs where typically only two would be allowed.

Special tower panels and custom light sconces were designed using painted perforated metals. New lighting fixtures were placed in the common areas and designed to produce the look of day, night and twilight at the center. Slate, used at column bases and bulkheads, unified the harmonious design.

The vacant Kmart was transformed into a state-of-the-art 10-screen cinema with all-stadium seating — one of the first California projects to convert a building into an all-stadium theater complex. A striking theme tower and neon-studded marquee reminiscent of downtown theaters gave it an unusual facade. The former outdoor Kmart sales area was converted into a theater cafe with its own outdoor dining patio.

High vacancy turned into high-impact design treatment with developer subsidy.

Each retailer has its own bold and creative signage — video, travel, banks.

The parking area was renovated as well, through resurfacing and reconfiguration, to provide more spaces, improved circulation and spaces for the handicapped. Trees in the lot were replaced with towering palms.

The center remained open during construction; the developer reports that sales even increased slightly during the work. An on-site employee acted as liaison between tenant, customers, the city and the developer to review progress and deal with problems. A construction phasing program ensured minimal disturbance to tenants and shoppers. Construction

From the multicolored neon logo of *The Manteca Marketplace* pylon (opposite center) to signs for restaurants and shops (above and right), lively graphics show the center has entered a new era.

With neon by night and canopies by day (below), The Manteca Marketplace achieved its goal of quality and drama in design.

areas were barricaded with lighted entries leading to stores. Security guards directed traffic and protected shoppers' safety.

Thousands of The Manteca Marketplace T-shirts, handbags and balloons with the center's new multicolored logo were distributed by tenants to customers, and several promotional events kept shoppers aware of the progress. The Manteca Marketplace proves that even a strip center that looks boarded up can realize its full potential.

Photos: Ronald Moore Photography

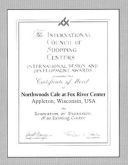

Owner:

General Growth Properties

Chicago, Illinois, United States

Architect/Designer:

Anthony Belluschi Architects, Ltd.

Chicago, Illinois, United States

Northwoods Cafe at Fox River Center

Appleton, Wisconsin, United States

Gross size of center:
980,982 sq. ft.

Gross leasable area excluding anchors:
386,068 sq. ft.

Type of center:
Regional center

Physical description:
Enclosed one-level mall with mezzanine at food court

Location of trading area:
Middle market

Population:
- Primary trading area
  348,300
- Secondary trading area
  620,900
- Annualized percentage of shoppers anticipated to be from outside trade area
  15%

Development schedule:
- Original opening date
  July 18, 1984
- Current expansion date
  November 1997

Parking spaces:
- Present number
  5,460

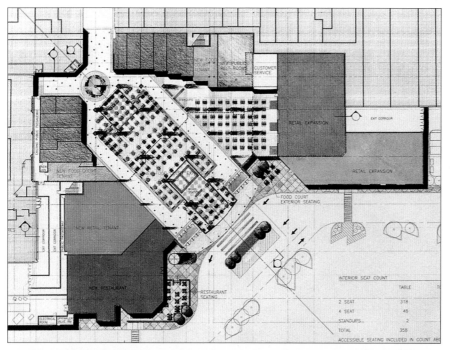

*S*hopper volume and length of time spent at Fox River Shopping Center had caused serious overcrowding in the food court and main entry areas. Although well maintained, after 15 years these locations needed a facelift and a new image. The existing stainless-steel-clad interior and 25-foot-high glazed office building facade were far too cold and institutional-looking for the friendly image the mall desired.

At Northwoods Cafe at Fox River Center, seating capacity (top) was more than doubled, to 850.

A 65-foot clerestory (above and right) rises over the food court and new entrance.

A drab, flat facade (far left) gave way to the attention-getting new entryway.

To give shoppers a sense of openness, the expansion doubled the seating capacity of the food court and added a full-service restaurant and a second entrance. The original 25-foot-high facade became a 65-foot-high gable-end clerestory with custom light chandeliers, stone and wood column cladding, a brick, stone and glazed curtain wall facade and a porcelain tile floor. The new facade brought spaciousness to the entry and food court, which displays poetry and photographs of local artists inspired by the northern Wisconsin woodlands.

Since the main entry was a central element of the renovation, traffic flow and shopper safety were key concerns during construction. The mall entry was shifted to an existing 20-foot-wide service corridor. A full-height barricade provided total isolation between shopper and construction; however, the public could view

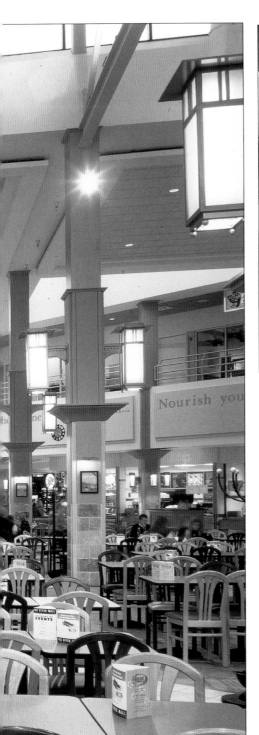

Larger in every direction than the old food court (above), the new one (opposite) is spacious and inviting.

Institutional-looking steel columns (near right) in the old food court were recovered in natural materials in the new family-focused food court (opposite page).

progress through vistas and portals. Part of the work was done overnight to minimize potential danger to shoppers.

As part of its renovation and expansion, the center began a new marketing campaign featuring a puppy as the mall's mascot, tying closely to the values of family, warmth and hospitality on which the project was based.

The developer credits close teamwork between owner, mall manager, on-site construction manager, architect and contractor as a principal reason for the success of the project. While communication with tenants was

ongoing, the developer believes a better job could have been done with one anchor in particular, which chose not to expand.

While little new leasable area was added, the renovation of Fox River Shopping Center's Northwoods Cafe added to the mall's appeal. Traffic flow improved, and the main entrance got a whole new look. The family-oriented center gained spacious restrooms and a new customer service area. The new clerestory-style facade provides the mall an attention-getting view from a nearby expressway, bringing visitors to the stores, food court and the 10-screen cinema.

MAJOR TENANTS		
NAME	**TYPE**	**GLA (SQ. FT.)**
Dayton's	Department store	168,800
Sears	Department store	127,606
Younkers	Department store	113,766
Target	Department store	100,750
JC Penney	Department store	83,992

Stone coverings on interior columns and lantern-like lighting create a village-like effect at Fox River Center.

Certificate of Merit

Owner:

Oak Park Investments, L.P.
c/o Copaken, White & Blitt
Leawood, Kansas, United States

Architect:

HNTB Corp.
Kansas City, Kansas, United States

Designer:

RTKL Associates Inc.
Dallas, Texas, United States

Oak Park Mall

Overland Park, Kansas, United States

Gross size of center:
1.5 million sq. ft.

Gross leasable area excluding anchors:
477,000 sq. ft.

Total acreage of site:
99 acres

Type of center:
Super-regional center

Physical description:
Enclosed mall

Location of trading area:
Suburban

Population:
- Primary trading area
  400,000
- Secondary trading area
  150,000
- Annualized percentage of shoppers
  anticipated to be from outside trade area
  20%

Development schedule:
- Original opening date
  August 1976
- Current expansion date
  March 1998

Parking spaces:
- Present number
  7,500

*N*ordstrom was the catalyst for the renovation and expansion of Oak Park Mall. While the center had very strong sales, low vacancy and a solid tenant mix, the addition of a Nordstrom store gave Oak Park the opportunity to more closely mirror its customers' tastes, preferences and lifestyles.

Oak Park's existing mid-1970s design lacked the personality and sense of place that today's shoppers have come to expect. Also, surface parking was only adequate.

In its renovation, Oak Park incorporated the images its name evokes: oak trees and forests. New oval-shaped courts feature clerestory windows and ceilings painted with oval leaf patterns in faux gold leaf. Plants abound at floor level and other locations. A playful touch was added in the design of a new pylon at the base of a stairway — it resembles the trunk of a tree, and a squirrel cutout scurries up the pylon toward a golden acorn atop the pole.

High priority was given to the architecture that the customer touches and sees. Wood is present in the top rails of patterned glass railings. Much of the design palette is tans and light greens, reflecting natural forest hues.

Oak Park's logo carries through the forest motif.

MAJOR TENANTS		
NAME	**TYPE**	**GLA (SQ. FT.)**
Dillards (two stores)	Department store	430,000
JC Penney	Department store	210,000
Nordstrom	Department store	205,000
Montgomery Ward	Department store	165,000

A plant feature, once encased in a bare planter (above) gets the full design treatment (top) in the renovation.

Lighting fixtures send diffused light throughout the mall area (right).

The developer says that the key to this successful project was that all parties — the City of Overland Park, Nordstrom, existing department stores and the owner — believed it was in their mutual business interests to commit the time, effort and money needed for the job. Perhaps most notable was the partnership between the owner and city government, which resulted in the city's construction of over 800 conveniently located structured public parking spaces. The parking improvements were funded through an Improvement District and will be paid for by future sales tax revenue generated by the mall.

The forest-and-leaves design image is expressed on light poles (right), the building facade (above), exterior signage and store directories (opposite page). Plantings abound at Oak Park Mall, on the food court floor and suspended above it. (opposite page top).

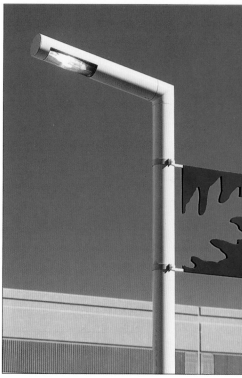

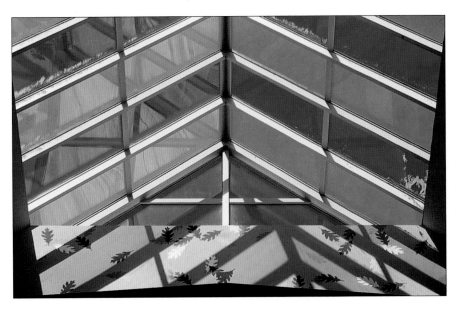

Since the mall would remain open during the renovation and expansion, construction was phased to minimize the impact on customer parking and vehicular circulation. Exterior work was shut down during the 1996 Christmas shopping season. Shopper safety was boosted by involving City Code and Fire Department officials early in the design process. Much of the interior work was done at night.

Skylights (right and below), in the mall area let the sun's rays reinforce the natural theme of the design concept.

The gentle palette of Oak Park Mall's redesign colors a courtyard (above) and the oval leaf patterns painted on ceilings (right).

A squirrel's relentness climb to get the acorn at the top is a playful sign of design element.

The addition of Nordstrom has attracted other new retailers as well: J. Crew, Rainforest Cafe, Ann Taylor, Eddie Bauer Premiere, Brookstone, Aceda, KCPT Store of Knowledge, Coach, Bailey Banks & Biddle, Johnny Rockets and others. Many stores are unique in the Kansas City area. Vacancy remains low despite the addition of 46,000 square feet of leasable space.

With a new Nordstrom and other prestige retailers, Oak Park advertised what else was new: a new floor, a new look, as well as new stores. The "New Oak Park" advertising program focused not just on current mall customers, but also on those who had not visited the mall since the expansion began.

Certificate of Merit

Owner:

Raffles City Pte. Ltd.
Singapore

Architect:

Architects 61 Pte. Ltd.
Singapore

Designer:

RTKL International Ltd.
Los Angeles, California, United States

Raffles City Shopping Centre

Singapore

Gross size of center:
260,000 sq. ft.

Gross leasable area excluding anchors:
150,914 sq. ft.

Total acreage of site:
7.57 acres

Type of center:
Regional fashion/Specialty center

Physical description:
Enclosed mall

Location of trading area:
Urban central business district

Population:
- Primary trading area
  3.74 million
- Annualized percentage of shoppers
  anticipated to be from outside trade area
  10%

Development schedule:
- Original opening date
  October 6, 1986
- Current expansion date
  October 1997

Parking spaces:
- Present number
  1,073
- 123 parking spaces deleted in
  renovation

*R*affles City Shopping Centre is part of the mixed-use Raffles City complex, which also includes a convention center, two hotels, one office tower and three below-grade parking levels. The center, designed by I. M. Pei, had been successful continuously since its opening in 1986, but the desire to stay at the forefront of the latest marketing trends and innovations prompted change.

Pei's designs tend to be monumental, geometric and highly abstract. A shopping center, however, needs a more welcoming personality. Renovation would include human-scale elements as well as additional leasable space.

The human scale included getting shoppers closer to the stores. The frontage of all shops facing the center of the atrium was pushed forward, placing storefronts closer to consumers and adding leasable space without increasing the gross building area.

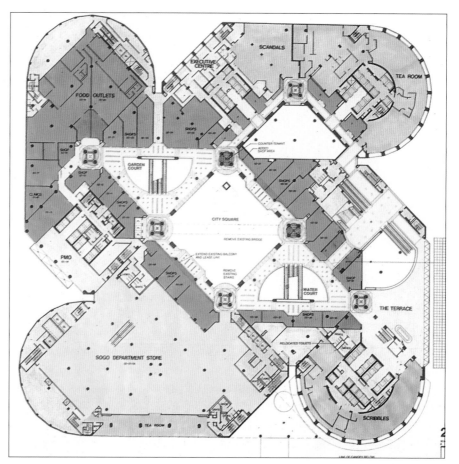

The City Square occupies the center of the Raffles plot view (above), flanked by the Garden Court and the Water Court.

Signs for the mall and its principal anchor welcome shoppers.

The center brings a glittery, high-tech look to the mixed-use project.

*The multilevel
Raffles City
Shopping Centre
has plenty of
vertical
transportation
(three photos, left).*

*Project goals
included bringing
human touches to
the immense scale.
Indoor plantings
help achieve this
objective.*

MAJOR TENANTS

NAME	TYPE	GLA (SQ. FT.)
SOGO	Department store	119,500
Food Junction	Food court	15,800
Esprit	Fashion retailer	10,300

Kiosks, escalators, water fountains and the newly created below-grade retail level are in easy view at Raffles City Shopping Centre.

Two interactive water features, among the first in the region, engage and delight shoppers. Adding to the atmosphere are three distinctly themed courts: the City Square, capturing Singapore's urban rhythms, and the Water Court and the Garden Court, which have abundant water elements and landscaping. The courts and the rest of the mall are infused with environmental graphics, which include poetry on the undersides of escalators.

During the 20-month renovation, the center remained fully open. Heavy or disruptive construction was carried out after shopping hours. Soundproof construction hoardings, decorated to lessen the visual impact of renovation, contained work done during mall hours. A marketing program sustained shopper traffic, and impact of the construction on business was minimal.

A floor plaque (above) defines The Marketplace, with its gourmet supermarket and eateries. Retailers were encouraged to make their storefronts more individualized (right).

Tenants were encouraged to re-do their storefronts in a more individual and creative fashion. A new baby/nursery room and other customer services were added. A basement area contains the new Marketplace, which features a gourmet supermarket and small eateries with free-form and eclectic storefronts. Reconfiguration of space allowed for a new 21-outlet food court.

Giant palms (opposite page and above) help shrink the enormous space to appreciable proportions. Column covers lend a touch of elegance to The Marketplace (right).

Pre-surveys and analysis of the center's needs aided in the identification and clear understanding of the goals and objectives of the renovation. These goals were communicated to the architect and tenants. The result was sales figures that increased, despite the general Asian economic malaise. The center won the Singapore Tourist Board award for best shopping experience. The award recognizes service standards, user-friendliness of infrastructure, innovative center concept and marketing, and tenant-management relationships.

Water features — among the first in Asian centers — are among the many visual excitements at Raffles City Shopping Centre (below).

Photos: Tim Griffith

Certificate of Merit

Owner:

Iguatemi Empresa de Shopping Centers SA, Nacional Iguatemi Ancar, Maiojama

São Paulo, SP, Brazil

Architect/Designer:

Beame Architectural Partnership

Coral Gables, Florida, United States

Shopping Center Iguatemi Porto Alegre

Porto Alegre, RS, Brazil

Gross size of center:
383,656 sq. ft.

Gross leasable area excluding anchors:
260,972 sq. ft.

Total acreage of site:
23.75 acres

Type of center:
Regional center

Physical description:
Enclosed two-level mall

Location of trading area:
Urban but not downtown

Population:
- Primary trading area
  400,000
- Secondary trading area
  200,000
- Annualized percentage of shoppers
  anticipated to be from outside trade area
  10%

Development schedule:
- Original opening date
  April 13, 1983
- Current expansion date
  October 30, 1997

Parking spaces:
- Present number
  3,015
- 1,015 parking spaces added

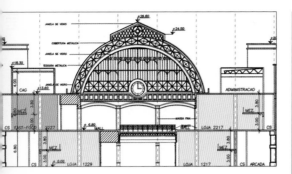

A dome tops the sectional view (left) of the entrance to the expansion of Shopping Center Iguatemi Porto Alegre (above).

Photo: Thomas Delbeck Photography

The expansion has an imposing exterior.

*T*he neighborhood around Shopping Center Iguatemi Porto Alegre had been increasing in population since the center opened in 1983. The economy had stabilized, and a growing middle class wanted higher quality stores and more leisure time activity. The center needed expansion to keep up with market demand, and renovation to discourage competition.

The center expanded in one direction: north, with an unbroken continuation of the existing mall. Transition from the existing to the new part of the center is seamless.

Improvements include new skylights, new lighting, architectural details and relief, second-level handrails and flooring. A new parking garage is open and bright, with very straightforward circulation. It is also one of the very few clear-span parking garages in Brazil.

The center boasts more cinema screens than any other location in Porto Alegre. One dynamic result of the expansion is that the center now has two multiscreen cinemas and two food courts. This serves to spread entertainment throughout the center and expands the center's clientele.

The main entry to the expansion (above) leads into the Renner anchor store, a dramatic improvement over an earlier entrance (right).

Photo: Thomas Delbeck Photography

A comparison of old (left) and new (above) demonstrates the importance of keeping a center's exterior up-to-date.

The center was kept open during the expansion. Phasing the work kept shops from closing. The new two-level Renner department store was constructed before the former Renner was converted into new small shops.

Opposite page: Skylights bring natural light through the center's many levels.

MAJOR TENANTS

NAME	TYPE	GLA (SQ. FT.)
Supermercado Real	Supermarket	15,385
Renner	Department store	10,699
C&A	Department store	9,482

Photo: Thomas Delbeck Photography

Excitement overhead, from unique lighting (left) to a ceiling dome (above).

The sun's path changes the center's lighting as the day wears on.

Photos: Thomas Delbeck Photography

Photo: Thomas Delbeck Photography

Sales volumes remained constant throughout the renovation. With the expansion, the shopping center's stores include fashion, housewares, groceries, full-line department stores, computers/electronics, hobbies, toys, sporting goods, cinemas, and both gourmet and fast-food restaurants. The developer is satisfied that there is no reason for shoppers to go elsewhere. A public relations and marketing campaign accompanied the renovation, followed by re-opening activities that attracted thousands.

Storefronts such as the one above keep pace with today's customer.

Date Due

BRODART, CO.   Cat. No. 23-233-003   Printed in U.S.A.